Since 1888, *National Geographic* magazine has provided its readers a wealth of information and helped us understand the world in which we live. Insightful articles, supported by gorgeous photography and impeccable research, bring the mission of the National Geographic Society front and center: to inspire people to care about the planet. The *Explore* series delivers *National Geographic* to you in the same spirit. Each of the books in this series presents the best articles on popular and relevant topics in an accessible format. In addition, each book highlights the work of National Geographic Explorers, photographers, and writers. Explore the world of *National Geographic*. You will be inspired.

ON THE COVER
Gray reef sharks and red snappers at Kingman Reef in the Pacific Ocean

Ocean Depths

Oceans are ever changing and always on the move. Tides rise and fall. Waves ripple gently or crash onto rocks. Flowing currents influence climates throughout the world. Oceans are critical to life on our planet. More than 97 percent of Earth's water is contained in oceans and seas. Humans depend on oceans for food, transportation, recreation, power, and even waste disposal.

Much of the ocean is still unknown and unexplored. Even in easier to reach areas such as Australia's Great Barrier Reef and the coast of northern California, scientists are still discovering new varieties of sea life and learning new things about how sea creatures survive and thrive there. In the depths, miles below the surface, the ocean world remains quiet, dark, and mysterious.

Some of the ocean's long-kept secrets are slowly being revealed. Improved cameras and robotic vehicles are making it possible to descend ever deeper. But just when new technologies are overcoming the challenges of ocean exploration, new pressures are endangering ocean life. Pollution and overdevelopment threaten the rich and complex environments, interfering with the natural, healthy process of renewal.

What can you do? Start by turning the pages of this book to experience the beauty of the undersea world. The articles are adapted from *National Geographic* magazine, and they support the mission of the National Geographic Society—to educate people about the plant, animal, and human life that shares our world. Read about strange and fascinating creatures, some as large as a whale, others as tiny as a microscopic organism. Meet dedicated explorers and scientists who study the ocean's depths. As you learn more, you may find yourself gaining a new respect for the world's oceans.

DRAGONS OF THE SEA
Two weedy sea dragons swim through seaweed. Sea dragons are native to the waters off southern and eastern Australia.

The *Great* Barrier Reef

BY JENNIFER S. HOLLAND

Adapted from "A Fragile Empire,"
by Jennifer S. Holland, in *National Geographic*, May 2011

FISHY CLOSEUP
The humped wrasse shares the Great Barrier Reef with many thousands of other species. This wrasse was not camera shy!

Parrotfish teeth grind against rock.
Sharks flash by. Tiny fish and shrimp
seem to dance as they guard their nooks.
This is the Great Barrier Reef.

STORY OF A REEF

The Great Barrier Reef's biological diversity
is part of what makes it great. It hosts 1,800
species of fish, 125 kinds of sharks, and countless
tiny organisms. But the most riveting sight of
all is the vast expanse of coral: small, marine
animals whose outer skeletons form wildly
interesting shapes—from staghorn stalks and
wave-smoothed plates to huge rocks draped with
leathery brown corals. The variety of animal
life that lives along the length of the reef is
unmatched in the world.

The reef's sheer size also makes it great. More
than 10,000 square miles of coral wind along the
ocean floor off Australia over a stretch of 1,400
miles. If the reef's main chunks were plucked
from the sea and laid out to dry, the rock could
cover all of New Jersey, with coral to spare.

Millions of years ago, time and tides and a
restless planet brought the Great Barrier Reef into
being. The same forces wore it down, and grew
it back—over and over again. Now all the factors
that let the reef grow are changing at a rate Earth
has never before experienced. This time the reef
may not be able to recover.

British explorer Captain James Cook
introduced Europeans to the Great Barrier Reef
off Australia. He came upon it quite by accident.
On a June evening in 1770, Cook heard the
screech of wood against stone. He didn't know it
at the time, but his ship had run into the most
massive living structure on Earth.

Cook and his team had been exploring the
waters off the coast of Australia when the ship hit
the reef. Not far beneath the surface of the water,
jagged towers of coral tore into the ship's hull and
held the vessel fast. Timbers splintered and the
sea poured in. The crew ran up on deck terrified
that the ship was about to sink. But captain and
crew managed to limp to a river mouth and patch
their ship.

Aborigines, native inhabitants of Australia, had
lived in the region for thousands of years before
European ships first hit the reef. Aboriginal
and Torres Strait Islander peoples had fished
the reef and shared myths about its creatures
for generations. The reef was part of their lives.
Historians, though, aren't sure what they knew
about the reef's structure and animal life. And
not until modern times did anyone know how
the great reef was formed.

EXPANSION AND EROSION

The Great Barrier Reef owes its existence to
organisms no bigger than a grain of rice.
Coral polyps, the reef's building blocks, are
actually animals that have algae, or tiny,
photosynthetic organisms in their cells. As those
algae photosynthesize—or use light to create
energy—each polyp secretes a "house" of calcium

BARRIER REEF
Wide ribbons of coral off Australia's northeastern coast form the largest coral reef ecosystem in the world.

carbonate, or limestone. As one house tops another, the colony expands like a city. Other marine life quickly grabs on and spreads, helping cement all the pieces together.

Corals grow best in shallow, clear, rough water with lots of light to support photosynthesis. Off Australia's eastern edge, conditions are right for this building of limestone walls. After millions of years of growing and changing, the reef stands as a jumble whose shapes, sizes, and life-forms are determined by where in the ocean they lie—how close to shore, for example—and what forces work on them, such as the pounding of waves. Far from the coast, where the light is low and the water is deeper, there's no reef at all.

"In the Great Barrier Reef, corals set the patterns of life from end to end," says Charlie Veron, coral expert and a chief scientist for the Australian Institute of Marine Science. With more than 400 species in the region, "they structure the entire environment. They're the **habitat** for everything else here." The perfect temperature, clarity, and currents enable some corals to grow rapidly. The reef continuously erodes as well. Waves, ocean chemistry, and organisms that eat limestone wear down the reef. This disappearing act is far slower than the constant building up. Over time, as much as 90 percent of the rock disappears into the waters, forming sand. The living exterior of this reef is ever changing.

At less than 10,000 years old, the underlying layers of the reef are relatively young. The reef's true beginnings go back 25 million years, Veron says, when coral **larvae** began riding south-flowing currents. The larvae grabbed footholds wherever they could. Slowly, colonies rich with marine life grew and spread along the sea floor.

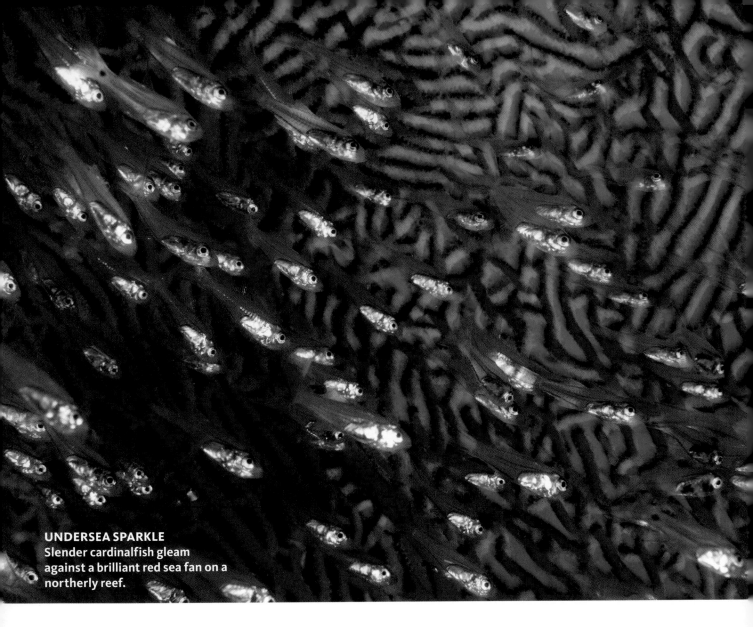

UNDERSEA SPARKLE
Slender cardinalfish gleam
against a brilliant red sea fan on a
northerly reef.

A CATALOG OF DISASTERS

Since the reef first started to form, ice ages have come and gone. The earth's plates have shifted. Ocean and atmospheric conditions have changed wildly. The reef has expanded and eroded, being torn down and rebuilt at nature's whim.

"A history of the Great Barrier Reef," Veron says, "is a catalog of disasters" caused by a changing planet. But they are disasters from which the reef has always recovered.

Today new disasters endanger the reef, and the prospect for recovery is uncertain. Recent rapid warming of the world's climate, scientists say, appears to be devastating for reefs. In corals, warming temperatures and increased exposure to the sun's rays lead to a stress response called bleaching. The colorful algae in coral cells become poisonous and are expelled. As it loses its algae, the host coral turns skeletal white.

Major bleaching in the Great Barrier Reef and elsewhere in 1997–98 was linked to record-high sea-surface temperatures. Another round began in 2001 and again in 2005. By 2030, some reef experts say, these destructive episodes will occur every year.

Heat may also be a reason for a 60-year decline in ocean phytoplankton. These microscopic organisms gobble **greenhouse gases** and feed, directly or indirectly, almost every other living thing in the sea. Changes in sea level, either up or down, have a dire impact as well. Decreasing sea levels expose shallow corals to too much sun. Higher levels drown them in deeper water, where they're hidden from the light.

A more immediate concern is massive flooding. In early 2011 floods on Australia's continent sent huge plumes of **sediment** and polluted waters onto the reef. The full harm to marine life won't be clear for years.

And then there's the acid test. During some periods in Earth's history, millions of years ago, greenhouse gases have increased in the atmosphere for natural reasons, such as heavy volcanic activity. Oceans absorbed these greenhouse gases, causing ocean acidity to rise. In time, high levels of acidity interfered with the ability of sea creatures to build their limestone shells and skeletons.

In some oceans acidity is rising again. The most vulnerable reef creatures are the calcium-excreting algae that help bind the reef. The more brittle the reef's bones, the more wave action, storms, diseases, pollutants, and other stresses can break them.

Veron paints a bleak picture of the Great Barrier Reef's future. He explains that in ancient times many corals adapted to changing ocean acidity. "The difference is there were long stretches in between. Corals had millions of years to work it out." He fears that high levels of industrial pollution and the increasing escape of methane, a greenhouse gas, as a result of Earth's melting ice will mean that much of the reef will be nearly dead within 50 years.

EDGING FORWARD

Two million tourists visit the Great Barrier Reef each year. They see an underwater paradise teeming with life. But the damage is there if you know where to look. The reef bears a two-mile-long scar from a collision with a Chinese coal carrier. Other ship groundings and occasional oil spills have marred the habitat. Sediment plumes from flooding and nutrients from agriculture and development also do very real damage to the **ecosystem**.

But Australians aren't likely to let the reef fall apart without a national outcry. One captain of a dive boat put it this way: "Without the reef, there's nothing out here but a whole lot of salty water." He added, "The reef is a loved one whose loss is too sad to contemplate." The reef is also crucial economically. The visitors he transports to the reef's edges add more than one billion dollars each year to Australia's economy.

The challenge is to keep the reef healthy despite rapid change. "To fix a car engine, you need to know how it works," says marine biologist Terry Hughes. "The same is true for reefs." He and others have been investigating how these ecosystems function so that efforts to prevent damage can be more effective.

High on the to-do list is to determine the full impact of overfishing. Traditionally, commercial fishermen could work along the reef. But with rising concern about big catches, the Australian government in 2004 set aside huge areas as off-limits to all fishing—including for sport. The biological recovery has been faster than expected. Within two years, for example, numbers of coral trout doubled on a once heavily fished reef. Some scientists believe protective zones may reduce outbreaks of a devastating coral-eating sea star.

Scientists also want to know what makes specific corals extra tough during times of change. "We know some reefs experience much more stressful conditions than others," says reef ecologist Peter Mumby. "Looking at decades of sea temperature data, we can now map where corals are most accustomed to

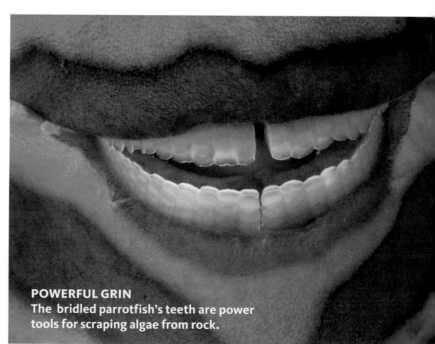

POWERFUL GRIN
The bridled parrotfish's teeth are power tools for scraping algae from rock.

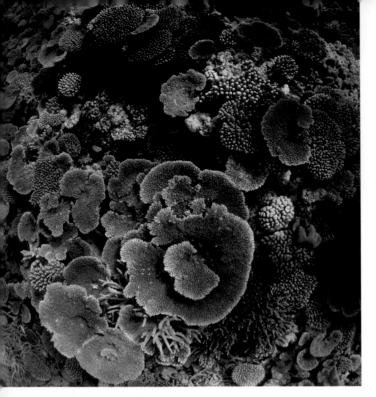

MASTER REEF BUILDERS
Tightly packed hard corals, mostly Acropora species, compete for space and energy-giving sunlight.

warmth and target conservation actions there." He says understanding how corals recover from bleaching—and figuring out where new polyps are likely to grow—can help in designing reserves. Even the outspoken Veron acknowledges that coral survival is possible long-term if the attacks on reefs are halted—soon.

Nature has some safeguards of her own that may have helped corals during past environmental disasters. One is hybridization—when different species mix genes. As Veron puts it, "Everything is always on its way to becoming something else." On the reef, about a third of the corals reproduce each year. During such events, as many as 35 species, with genetically different parents, are reproducing at the same time and mingling in the same waters. "This provides outstanding opportunities to produce hybrids," explains marine biologist Bette Willis. With climate and ocean chemistry in such **flux**, she says, hybridization can offer a speedy path to hardiness against disease.

Despite today's serious threats, the Great Barrier Reef won't easily crumble. It has, after all, survived catastrophic change before. And all kinds of marine life are around to help keep the reef whole. For example, in studies conducted in 2007, scientists found that where grazing fish thrive, so do corals. The scientists believe that if vegetarian fish with big appetites are protected, then corals also can prevail.

A human visitor to the reef can see the fish doing their vital job. In dappled afternoon light, high walls of coral tower over a rare species of batfish. Long-finned and masked in black, the fish nibbles back strands of seaweed. And a school of parrotfish—with teeth like wire cutters—chip away noisily at the rocks, where mats of green and red algae have quietly taken hold. Life goes on in the Great Barrier Reef.

THINK ABOUT IT! ||||||||||||||||||||||||||||||||||||

1 **Describe Geographic Information** The Great Barrier Reef was named for very specific reasons. Explain what makes it a "reef," what makes the reef "great," and in what ways it is a "barrier."

2 **Make Predictions** Do you think the reef will survive? Support your prediction with reasons based on information in this article.

3 **Synthesize** Describe the process of forming coral. How is the health of coral critical to the health of the entire reef?

BACKGROUND & VOCABULARY

ecosystem *n.* (EE-koh-sihs-tuhm) a community of organisms interacting with their natural environment

flux *n.* a state of constant change

greenhouse gases *n.* the gases in the atmosphere that trap heat and contribute to global warming

habitat *n.* (HAB-uh-tat) the environment where an animal naturally lives or once lived

larvae *n.* (LAHR-vee) the early, often wormlike forms of animals

sediment *n.* (SEHD-ih-muhnt) the material such as sand, mud, and rocks that is deposited in water

Relics to Reefs

BY STEPHEN HARRIGAN

Adapted from "Relics to Reefs," by Stephen Harrigan,
in *National Geographic*, February 2011

A REEF GROWS UP
Steel pillars supporting
a drilling platform
make an artificial reef
in the Gulf of Mexico.

It took just over two minutes for the *General Hoyt S. Vandenberg* to sink to the bottom of the Atlantic off Key West, Florida. The 46 explosive charges placed inside the ship blew, and the ship gracefully slipped beneath the surface. Over time, the *Vandenberg* would turn into an artificial reef, another new destination for divers and anglers.

BECOMING A REEF

The *Vandenberg* is not the first ship to be sunk deliberately to create an artificial reef. The waters off the Florida Keys are the gravesite of two Coast Guard cutters and a U.S. Navy landing ship. On the sandy bottom 20 or so miles out to sea from Pensacola lies an entire aircraft carrier, the largest ship ever to be sunk as an artificial reef. Dozens of World War II cargo ships have been sunk along the U.S. coasts.

People around the world have long known that shipwrecks are prime fishing sites. As early as the 1830s, American fishermen were building artificial reefs out of logs. In our own time most do-it-yourself reefs have been made out of junk: refrigerators, shopping carts, rusting cars, vending machines. Pretty much anything that sinks can become an artificial reef. Even "official" reefs are often created from odd materials: retired subway cars, old battle tanks, armored cars, and oil drilling rigs, for example.

Many factors determine how—or whether—a human-made hulk can become an undersea garden. Depth, water temperature, currents, and the make-up of the sea bottom are all variables.

In contrast, sea life takes over artificial reefs in more predictable stages. First, a current comes up against a structure. The encounter creates an upwelling, or rising column, of water. The water is rich in **plankton** and becomes a reliable feeding spot for sardines and minnows. These small fish attract **predators** such as blue-fin tuna and sharks. Next come the creatures looking for protection from the dangers of the open ocean. These creatures seek out holes and crevices. They include groupers, snapper, squirrelfish, and eels. Predators such as jack and barracuda then take up stations where they wait for their **prey** to show themselves. In time, life will be sprouting everywhere.

Many species of fish seek shelter in the underwater structures of oil and gas platforms. For decades platforms in the Gulf of Mexico have been prime sites for sportfishing. "The economic benefit of artificial reefs is very clear," says Michael Miglini, the captain of a boat often hired by anglers in search of good fishing. He continues, "An artificial reef is a way of boosting the ocean's capacity to create fish, to increase the life of the Gulf."

Some biologists worry that artificial reefs simply attract fish from natural reefs. They are also concerned that the new reefs may become killing zones for popular fish such as red snapper. The snapper is one of the Gulf's most harvested game fish. It could be one of the species with the most to gain by having new reef habitats.

"When it comes to red snappers, artificial reefs are bait," says James H. Cowan, Jr., a professor of oceanography and coastal sciences. "If success is judged solely by an increase in harvest, then artificial reefs are pretty successful. But if those structures . . . are pulling fish off natural reefs farther from the coast, they may actually be increasing the overfishing of species that are already under stress."

Artificial reefs can pose other problems. Some steadily leak toxins into the surrounding waters for years. Because of the danger of pollution, almost 70 percent of the *Vandenberg's* sinking budget went to cleanup efforts. Workers removed more than 10 tons of asbestos and more than 800,000 feet of electrical wire. Nowadays, reefs must be created following the strict rules set out in the government's National Artificial Reef Plan.

NEW LIFE FOR AN OLD SHIP
Covered with colorful sponges and corals, the sunken U.S. Coast Guard Cutter *Duane* attracts both fish and divers.

REEFS GONE WRONG

Even well planned projects can go very wrong. One Navy ship sunk off Key Largo landed upside down. Parts of the ship projected above the waterline, ready to serve as a can opener to ships cruising over her. It took a massive effort to get her over on her side and fully underwater. Three years later, Hurricane Dennis finally moved her completely into position.

Despite her problems, this ship ended up a success story. Not so for the Osborne Tire Reef project in the early 1970s. In one win-win stroke, up to two million old tires would leave the landfills to create a thriving marine habitat.

It turned out, though, that the rubber in tires is a poor support for coral growth. The bundled tires did not form a new extension of two side-by-side natural reefs, as the planners intended. Instead the falling tires ended up smothering and bashing into the existing reefs' fragile organisms. When the bundles broke apart, the tires washed up on the nearby beaches. The once hopeful reef project has now been replaced by the Osborne Reef Waste Tire Removal Project.

THINK ABOUT IT! ||||||||||||||||||||||||||||||||

1 **Compare and Contrast** How is an artificial reef different from a natural reef? How are these two types of reefs the same?

2 **Sequence Events** What are the main events in the marine life takeover of an artificial reef?

BACKGROUND & VOCABULARY

plankton *n.* (PLANK-tuhn) tiny floating animal and plant life

predator *n.* (PREHD-uh-tuhr) an animal that gets its food mainly from killing and eating other animals

prey *n.* an animal that is food for another animal

UNDERWATER PALS
Undaunted by his companion's size, this man swims with a whale shark in the Indian Ocean off the coast of Mozambique.

Whale Sharks Get Social

BY JENNIFER S. HOLLAND

Adapted from "Sharing with Sharks," by Jennifer S. Holland,
in *National Geographic*, October 2011

The biggest fish in the sea is as long as a school bus, weighs as much as 50,000 pounds, and has a mouth that looks, head-on, wide enough to suck down a small car.

SHARKS, NOT WHALES

Scientists know very little about this species of shark, aptly called the whale shark. Whale sharks are generally loners, but in one corner of Indonesia, several miles off Papua, New Guinea, groups gather year-round. They zip by one another, nose around for handouts near the surface, and yank on fishing nets trying to make off with the day's catch. In other words, the giant fish act like the rest of the sharks. Scientists are studying the Indonesian whale sharks in hopes of learning more about the mysterious species.

These giants are indeed sharks, not whales. They breathe through gills, like fish. They are cold-blooded, like fish. The "whale" part of the name refers to size and how the animals eat. They are one of only three known shark species that filter feed, like some whales do.

Whale sharks swim slowly with jaws wide open through waters that are rich in tiny floating organisms called plankton. Water goes in carrying edibles of all sizes. Water flows out minus the food. A typical adult whale shark cruises at a relaxed one to three miles an hour. It must move night and day to take in enough water to feed itself.

The colossal fish is hard to study partly because it is hard to find and track. By tagging individual sharks, scientists have learned that the fish can log thousands of miles in years-long trips. But they sometimes disappear for weeks, diving more than a mile down and resting in the chilly deep. No one has ever found the whale sharks' mating or birthing grounds.

From the Indonesian sharks, and from the local fishermen who interact with them daily, scientists are learning about these giants of the ocean. They are working to identify each shark by its markings, preparing to launch studies of the beasts. For now, just being near them is exciting. Photographer Michael Aw describes the experience. "You are sandwiched in, sharks ahead and behind, but you want to be there. They make eye contact with you and then charge by. It blows your mind."

THINK ABOUT IT! ||||||||||||||||||||||||||||||||

Analyze Visuals Choose one of the photographs and write a new caption that applies information in the article to what is shown in the photo.

TIME FOR LUNCH
Whale sharks feed from fishing nets off the coast of Indonesia. Inset: Viewed head-on, a whale shark seems to be all mouth.

PHOTOGRAPHER'S JOURNAL

with **Brian J. Skerry**

FRIENDLY COEXISTENCE
Oceanic whitetip sharks have a reputation of eating humans stranded at sea. Skerry captured this nine-foot whitetip as it swam past fellow photographer Wes Pratt in the Bahamas. Good news: everyone survived.

UNDERWATER OBSERVER
Aboard a fishing vessel off the coast of Cape Breton, Canada, Skerry prepares to dive into icy waters to photograph leatherback turtles.

Brian Skerry is a National Geographic photographer who specializes in marine wildlife and underwater environments. Skerry's images show the mystery and beauty of the sea. They also help bring attention to our endangered oceans and their inhabitants.

Because of his nearly year-round assignment schedule, Skerry frequently finds himself in environments of extreme contrast—including tropical reefs and the waters beneath polar ice. While on assignment he has lived on the bottom of the sea, spent months aboard fishing boats, and traveled in everything from snowmobiles to canoes to the Goodyear blimp to get the shot.

Skerry has photographed the harp seal's struggle to survive in frozen waters, the last remaining pristine coral reefs, and the plight of the endangered right whale. His stories span the diversity of sea life.

After three decades of exploring the world's oceans, Brian Skerry continues to pursue stories that will increase awareness about the sea: "The oceans are in trouble. . . . My hope is to continually find new ways of creating images and stories that both celebrate the sea yet also highlight environmental problems. Photography can be a powerful instrument for change."

CURIOUS EEL
A moray eel slithers
through branches of
soft coral near the Izu
Peninsula, Honshu, Japan.

COLORFUL JELLYFISH
This multicolored jellyfish, called a mauve stinger, floats in sunlit Atlantic waters off the coast of Ireland.

HUNGRY LOGGERHEAD
A loggerhead turtle munches on sea grass in the waters off the coast of Belize in Central America.

THINK ABOUT IT! |||||||||||||||||||||||||||||||||||

1 **Pose and Answer Questions** What questions would you like to ask Brian Skerry about his work? How do you think you might find some answers to your questions?

2 **Synthesize** Think about what you have learned in this article and others you have read in this book. Why is understanding the ocean important to people?

Brimming Pools

BY MEL WHITE

Adapted from "Brimming Pools," by Mel White,
in *National Geographic*, June 2011

AT THE EDGE OF THE OCEAN
The sea washes out to reveal the
species that live on the edge of
Bodega Bay, California.

A narrow strip of shoreline along the northern California coast is an intertidal zone, a place where sea creatures are covered and uncovered by tides each day. At low tide, rocks and pools emerge, teeming with life. Writer Mel White took a tour of this amazing ecosystem and shared his impressions.

TIDE POOL PREDATOR

Pisaster ochraceus—the sea star—is one of the most impressive creatures inhabiting the shores near Bodega Bay, 65 miles north of San Francisco. Sometimes a foot across, sometimes orange and sometimes purple, the sea star is usually found resting in the crack of a rock. It looks like a lazy creature. But the sea star, also sometimes called the starfish, is a top predator of the **intertidal** zone, even though it has nothing that resembles a brain.

Sarah Ann Thompson, a marine biologist, is guiding me over the rugged rocks and through the tide pools of Bodega Head's Mussel Point. She stoops to pick up an orange sea star. As the result of an amazing **adaptation**, the sea star can, in a heartbeat, turn the soft tissues in its normally limp body into a structure as solid as bone. The star can then grab the shells of a mussel with hundreds of sucker-like feet and pull them apart. The star in Thompson's hand has a mussel in its clutches.

"This *Pisaster* has already killed the mussel," Thompson says, holding the sea star and the mussel in one hand and separating the mussel's shells a bit with the other. "[It has pushed] its stomach out through its mouth. And it's digesting the mussel externally."

So that goo inside the mussel . . . ?

"Yes, that's the *Pisaster*'s stomach. When it's finished eating, it pulls its stomach back inside itself and goes on its way."

A CONCENTRATED WORLD

The intertidal zone is a small model of ecological processes that happen on much larger scales. Biologists who study life zones—the way plants and animals change from the desert up to mountain peaks—must travel many miles to experience a wide range of habitats. The intertidal zone displays the same type of range: from the sea grass at the bottom up through layers of sea anemones and mussels and barnacles up to the limpets at the top. The difference is that all these habitats are found within a few steps of each other.

When a tornado rips through a mature forest, centuries will pass as grasses grow, then give way to shrubs and the forest eventually renews itself. But when a patch of intertidal life gets scraped down to the bare rock, biologists can watch life return practically before their eyes. The cycle of renewal lasts just a few years.

The rocks and pools here host as much diversity as any rain forest. The sea star is just one of numerous species that have adapted to the **micro habitats**. These species display a seemingly endless variety of physical shapes and lifestyles. One little worm can shoot a harpoon out of its head to stab its prey. A limpet tends and guards its own farm plot. A seaweed releases acid for defense when it's injured.

DIVERSE LIFE
Three forms of life display the variety to be found in California's intertidal zone: a fuzzy hooded shrimp (top), a lined chiton mollusk (middle), and fish eggs (bottom).

STRANGE STAR
The six-armed star lives in intertidal zones all along the U.S. West Coast. This star has lost an arm.

HUNGRY STARS
Predatory sea stars move between gooseneck barnacles and sea anemones in a tide pool.

Why all the aggression? It's simply the result of plants and animals competing for resources in a highly productive but limited space. In nature, as in real estate, location is everything, and the intertidal zone is like an elegant neighborhood in a world-class city.

SURPRISING CREATURES

A couple days later, I'm rock-hopping above Horseshoe Cove, a notch in Bodega Bay, with Jackie Sones, a researcher from the Bodega Marine Reserve. "This," she says, holding up a pale orange creature about the size of her fingernail, "is . . . a sea spider." Through a hand lens, it does in fact look like a spider, although one with body and legs ribbed and puffy.

"It uses its **proboscis** to puncture sea anemones and suck out fluids," Sones says. But this tiny predator has a nurturing side. Sones turns the sea spider over to reveal a cluster of tiny whitish eggs. "The males care for the developing young," she says.

The development of intertidal creatures varies nearly as much as their physical forms. Many go through a free-swimming larval stage that lasts weeks or months. They venture into the immense ocean before settling down as adults on a patch of rock.

We kneel to examine one of those larval roamers—or rather the resulting adult. The giant green sea anemone is a fearsome predator. Rather than actually hunting, though, it waits for unsuspecting prey to wander within reach. Resembling a blob of lime gelatin out of the water, the sea anemone blooms when submerged. It extends delicate tentacles outward and swallows its prey whole. Like jellyfish, sea anemones use stinging structures. They fire them like microscopic darts to stun prey.

Once they've set up housekeeping, sea anemones and many of their neighbors in the intertidal zone live long lives. In laboratories, sea anemones have lived decades without showing any signs of aging. Some in the wild are believed to be 150 years old or more.

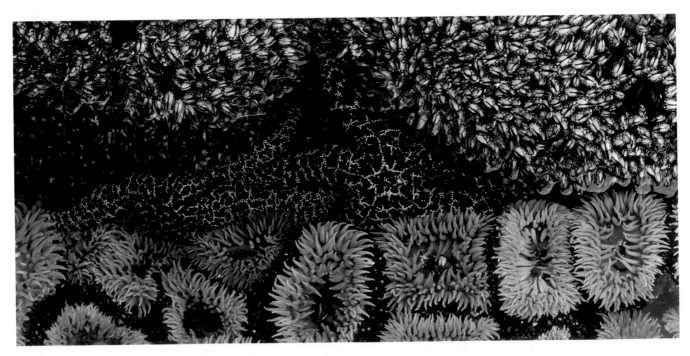

NOW YOU SEE IT, NOW YOU DON'T
Left: The shoreline at Fitzgerald Marine Reserve in California is covered by water at high tide.
Right: When the Fitzgerald shoreline is at low tide, people can observe sea life in the tidal pools.

A CHANGING ENVIRONMENT

Biologists question how even highly adaptable intertidal plants and animals will respond to new threats. These include pollution and **silt** washing off the coast. In addition, harvesting of some seaweeds has increased.

Of far greater importance is the increasing acidity of the ocean caused by higher levels of carbon dioxide in the atmosphere. Mollusks, crustaceans, and even some algae are among the living things that use calcium in their structures. Higher acidity levels in seawater could interfere with the production of calcium. Rising ocean temperatures are also a threat. Warm water holds less oxygen than cold water.

Thinking about the interconnectedness of life, Steinbeck wrote, "It is advisable to look from the tide pool to the stars and then back to the tide pool again." As a **microcosm** of the ocean—the nursery of all life—the intertidal zone is like an entire galaxy, one easily within our grasp.

THINK ABOUT IT! ||||||||||||||||||||||||||||||||

1 **Make Inferences** How does a microcosm like an intertidal zone help scientists understand environmental processes?

2 **Categorize** Which organisms in the article are predators? Which organisms are prey?

3 **Make Generalizations** Based on the information in this article, do you think climate change will have an effect on other ecosystems also? Why or why not?

BACKGROUND & VOCABULARY

adaptation *n.* (a-dap-TAY-shuhn) an adjustment to environmental conditions

intertidal *adj.* describing seashore that is covered and uncovered by tides each day

micro habitat *n.* a small, specific environment within a larger habitat

microcosm *n.* (MY-kroh-khaz-um) a little version of a larger world

proboscis *n.* (pruh-BAHS-kuhs) an extendible, tube-shaped structure on an animal's face that can act as a mouth or a nose

silt *n.* the fine particles of soil, rock, and minerals deposited by the flow of water, wind, and ice

Unseen **Titanic**

BY HAMPTON SIDES

Adapted from "Unseen Titanic," by Hampton Sides, in *National Geographic*, April 2012

At 2:20 a.m. on April 15, 1912, the "unsinkable" Titanic *disappeared beneath the waves, taking with her some 1,500 lives. Writer Hampton Sides talked with some of the people who discovered the long-lost wreck of the great ship.*

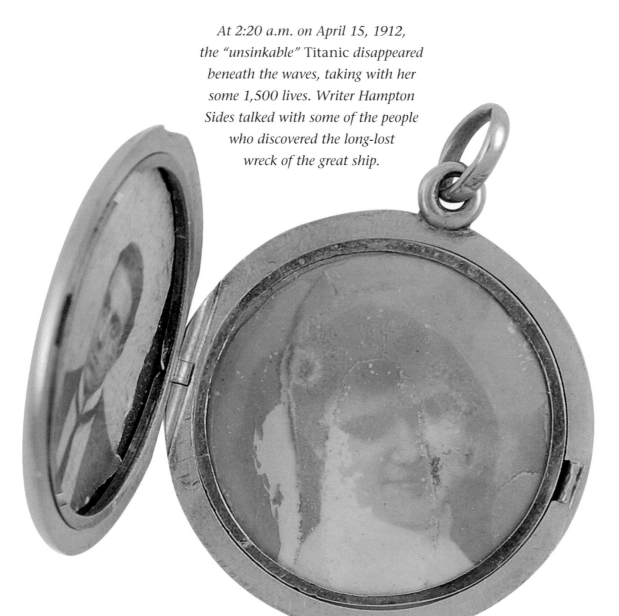

PICTURES OF LOSS
This locket was recovered from the body of a passenger who drowned.

SETTING OUT
The *Titanic* sails away from the dock at either Belfast, Ireland, where it was built, or Southampton, England, from where it set out on its first and only voyage.

A COMPLETE PICTURE AT LAST

For most of the 20th century, the *Titanic* slept in darkness, its corroded steel scattered across a thousand acres of the North Atlantic seabed. The ship's wreckage was discovered in 1985. Since then, explorers have been bringing back increasingly vivid pictures of it. Yet we've mainly glimpsed the site as through a keyhole, the view limited by the lights of a robot vehicle. Never have we taken the full measure of what's down there. Until now.

In a trailer on a back lot of the Woods Hole Oceanographic Institution, William Lange stands over a blown-up **sonar** map of the *Titanic* site. At first glance the ghostly image looks like the surface of the moon. On closer inspection, though, the site appears to be littered with human-made debris. Lange points to a portion of the map that has been brought to life by layering optical data onto the sonar image. He zooms in, and in, and in again. Now we can see the *Titanic*'s bow, or front section, in gritty clarity. We see a gaping black hole where a funnel (a kind of smokestack) once sprouted and a hatch cover resting in the mud a few hundred feet away. The

image is rich in detail. In one frame we can even make out a white crab clawing at a railing. Here, in the sweep of a computer mouse, we can see the entire wreck of the *Titanic*. "Now we know where everything is," Lange says. "After a hundred years, the lights are finally on."

The imagery we were seeing was the result of an ambitious multimillion-dollar expedition undertaken in August–September 2010. The images were taken by three state-of-the-art robotic vehicles flying at various altitudes above the seafloor. The robots bristled with sonar devices and high-definition cameras snapping hundreds of images a second. The ribbons of data they recorded have now been digitally stitched together into a massive high-definition picture.

"This is a game-changer," says archaeologist James Delgado, the expedition's chief scientist. "In the past, trying to understand *Titanic* was like trying to understand [New York City] at midnight in a rainstorm—with a flashlight. Now we have a site that can be understood and measured. . . . In years to come this historic map may give voice to those people who were silenced, seemingly forever, when the cold water closed over them."

WHY THE FASCINATION?

Why, a century later, do people still give so much attention to this graveyard of metal more than two miles beneath the ocean surface?

For some it's the extremes: a ship so strong and so grand, sinking in water so cold and so deep. Others are fascinated with the people on board, with the 2,208 individual stories that unfolded as the ship sank. Most passengers behaved honorably, and some were heroic. The captain stayed at his post. The band played on. The radio operators sent distress signals until the very end.

Something else went down with the *Titanic*: the optimism of the period before World War I. "The *Titanic* disaster was the bursting of a bubble," filmmaker and explorer James Cameron told me. "There was such a sense of bounty in the first decade of the 20th century. . . . Everything seemed so wondrous, on an endless upward spiral. Then it all came crashing down."

Since 1994, RMS Titanic, Inc. (RMST) has been the wreck's legal **salvager**. The company has exhibited artifacts from the Titanic in 20 countries around the world. I spent a mid-October day wandering among the relics. They included mostly ordinary objects: a razor, lumps of coal, a set of dishes, pairs of shoes, bottles of perfume. They are made extraordinary by the long, terrible journey that brought them to these clean display cases.

The exhibit's centerpiece was a gigantic slab of *Titanic*'s hull, known as the "big piece," which weighs 15 tons. This monstrosity of black metal reminded me of a dinosaur in

HIGH TEA
First-class passengers used this china teacup later recovered in the wreckage of the ship.

a museum: impossibly huge, pinned and braced at great expense, an extinct species from a lost world.

In recent years, RMST has shifted its focus away from salvaging and exhibiting artifacts toward being part of a long-term plan for approaching the wreck as an archaeological site.

Recently RMST hired one of the world's top *Titanic* experts to analyze the 2010 images. Bill Sauder's business card identifies him as a "director of *Titanic* research." When I met Sauder in Atlanta, he was parked at his computer, trying to make sense of a heap of rubbish near the *Titanic*'s stern, or back section.

Sauder soon zoomed in on an image. Within a few minutes he had identified the crumpled brass frame of a revolving door. Only someone who knows every inch of the ship could have recognized this small a piece of the enormous *Titanic* puzzle.

DEATH OF THE *TITANIC*

In late October of 2011 I found myself inside a huge film studio surrounded by props from James Cameron's 1997 movie, *Titanic*. Now he had called together a group of the world's foremost *Titanic* experts for a two-day meeting on the sinking of the ship. Cameron is an expert himself, having led three expeditions to the site, including a 1995 visit to shoot footage for his movie. Participants focused on a few questions: Why did the *Titanic* break up the way she did? Exactly where did the hull fail? At what angle did the wreckage smash into the seabed?

Listening to the discussions, I had one overwhelming impression. The *Titanic*'s final moments were hideously, horrifically violent. Many accounts describe the ship as "slipping beneath the ocean waves." Nothing could be further from the

BEFORE AND AFTER
This photograph of the interior of a first-class private suite (above, left) reveals the luxury that some *Titanic* passengers enjoyed. An underwater view of a first-class cabin (above, right) shows how time and water have preserved a once-grand space.

truth. Using analysis, models, and **simulations**, the experts painted a far more gruesome picture.

From the moment the ship hit the iceberg at 11:40 p.m., sinking was a certainty. By 2:18 a.m., with the last lifeboat having departed, the *Titanic* cracked in half. The ship's bow shot for the bottom, gaining speed as it dropped, and parts began to tear away. The bow hit with such massive force that you can still see the pattern of sand it displaced on the seafloor.

The stern, separated from the bow, descended even more traumatically. A large forward section completely came apart, spitting its contents into the depths.

Listening to the account of the *Titanic*'s death, I kept wondering: What happened to the people still on board as she sank? Most of the 1,496 victims died in the cold water at the surface, still in their cork life preservers. But hundreds

of people may have been alive inside. How did they, during their last moments, experience the break-up of the ship? What would they have heard and felt? It was, even a hundred years later, too awful to think about.

THINK ABOUT IT! ||||||||||||||||||||||||||||||

1 **Summarize** In your own words, explain why the *Titanic* still fascinates people today.

2 **Make Inferences** William Lange says, "After a hundred years, the lights are finally on." What does he mean?

3 **Find Main Ideas and Details** The author describes the *Titanic*'s final moments as as "hideously, horrifically violent." What details in the article support this conclusion?

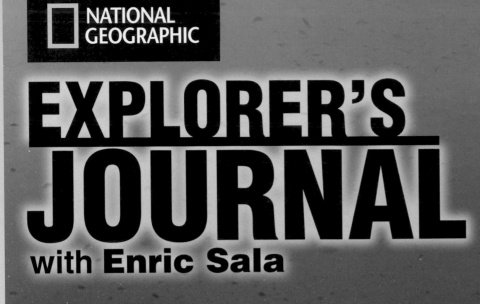

EXPLORER'S JOURNAL

with Enric Sala

REEF ENCOUNTERS
Sala observes a Mediterranean dusky grouper at the Medes Islands Marine Reserve, Spain.

Today, Enric Sala is a National Geographic Explorer, a marine ecologist, and a respected scientist and conservationist. But he first fell in love with the sea as a boy growing up along the Mediterranean coast of Spain. Witnessing the harm done to those waters led him to dedicate his life to preserving marine ecosystems throughout the world.

IN HIS OWN WORDS

As a child, I learned to snorkel before I knew how to swim. My first clear memory is of seeing a red starfish one summer off Spain's Costa Brava. My family's experience with fish was mostly on the stove—they ran a restaurant. But I watched the documentaries of the great ocean explorer and filmmaker Jacques-Yves Cousteau and dreamed of being a diver on his ship.

PRESERVING REEFS
The pristine coral reef of Ducie Atoll, Pitcairn Islands, South Pacific

I assumed as a child that big fish belonged only to exotic, tropical seas. I didn't see them in the Mediterranean I knew. But years later, in that same sea's Medes Islands Marine Reserve, I finally saw all the fish I'd never seen before: sea bream, corvina, grouper. I saw all that had been lost to overfishing and pollution and realized that the whole Mediterranean must once have been like this.

That is when I decided to work on creating marine reserves. These protected areas benefit fish and people. After many years, sea life can recover to levels similar to those in pristine areas. Fishermen gain too. At one Kenya fishery, on the eastern coast of Africa, incomes have doubled because of marine reserves.

In recent years I've helped inspire leaders to create marine protected areas off Chile, Costa Rica, Belize, and the United States. But more needs to be done to restore ocean health. We need to better manage our unsustainable fisheries, improve our methods of raising fish for food, and enforce marine-pollution laws.

My happiest moments are underwater, especially in places with large predators. If there are predators, it means there is more of everything, and I know the waters are healthy.

THINK ABOUT IT! ||||||||||

Analyze Cause and Effect What experiences inspired Enric Sala to become a marine scientist?

Document-Based Question

Oceans matter. But human activities are threatening their survival. People have used them as dumping grounds for chemicals and trash. They have also overfished certain types of fish. In response, many National Geographic Explorers and oceanographers, or scientists who study the oceans, are taking steps to preserve and protect them.

DOCUMENT 1 Primary Source

Oceans in Trouble

Sylvia Earle is a National Geographic Explorer and an oceanographer who has spent much of her life studying the world's oceans and working for their protection. Her work has earned her the title "Hero for the Planet." In the following excerpt, Earle explains how oceans provide our life-support system.

> The report that the ocean is in trouble is no surprise. What is shocking is that it has taken so long for us to make the connection between the state of the ocean and everything we care about—the economy, health, security—and the existence of life itself. . . . Photosynthetic organisms [plants that change light into energy] in the sea yield most of the oxygen in the atmosphere, take up and store vast amounts of carbon dioxide, shape planetary chemistry, and hold the planet steady. Even if you never see the ocean, your life depends on its existence. With every breath you take, every drop of water you drink, you are connected to the sea.

from "If the Sea Is in Trouble, We Are All in Trouble," by Sylvia Earle, independent.co.uk.com, June 21, 2011

CONSTRUCTED RESPONSE

1. According to Earle, how do the oceans serve as our life-support system?

DOCUMENT 2 Primary Source

Benefits of Marine Reserves

National Geographic Explorer and oceanographer Enric Sala works to establish marine reserves, which are protected areas off limits to fishing. In this excerpt, Sala describes the multiple benefits of marine reserves.

> There are benefits inside and outside the boundaries of marine reserves. Inside, fish and other marine life increase their [abundance]. Outside the reserve boundaries, some of these fish spill over. This spillover replenishes local fish populations, which helps local fishermen. Inside the reserve there is often a boost in tourism. There are few places where there are still lots of fish, so people flock to these places.
>
> Our studies show that a reserve's value can be greater than its pre-reserve value in as little as five years. So reserves not only have environmental benefits in terms of protecting biodiversity, but they are also a good business.

from "New Research: Marine Reserves Can Stoke Local Economies," by Brian Clark Howard, newswatch. nationalgeographic.com, April 3, 2013

CONSTRUCTED RESPONSE

2. What are some of the benefits of marine reserves?

Why are oceans important and
what are oceanographers
doing to protect them?

DOCUMENT 3 Secondary Source

Earth's "Hope Spots"

In 2009 Sylvia Earle launched a program called Mission Blue, which seeks to heal and protect Earth's oceans. A key goal of the program is the establishment of the "hope spots" shown on this map. These spots are ocean habitats that can recover and grow if human impact is limited.

CONSTRUCTED RESPONSE

3. What pattern do you notice in the locations of most of the hope spots?

PUT IT TOGETHER

Review Think about your responses to the Constructed Response questions and what you've learned about oceans from this book. Consider the impact of human activities on the oceans. Also, recall the ways in which oceans benefit people and Earth.

List Main Idea and Details Jot down each document's main idea and details. Remember that the main idea is the subject of a text. Details support and clarify the main idea.

Write Write a topic sentence that answers this question: Why are oceans important and what are oceanographers doing to protect them? Then write a paragraph that supports your topic sentence using evidence from the documents.

INDEX

||||||||||||||||||||||||||||||||||||||||||||||||||

SKILLS